WHO WAS...?

Isambard Kingdom Brunel

Kay Barnham

First published in 2007 by Wayland
Copyright © Wayland 2007

Wayland
338 Euston Road
London NW1 3BH

Wayland Australia
Level 17/207 Kent Street
Sydney, NSW 2000

Editor: Victoria Brooker
Designer: Jane Stanley

Barnham, Kay
    Who was Isambard Kingdom Brunel?
    1. Brunel, Isambard Kingdom, 1806-1859 - Juvenile
literature 2. Civil engineers - England - Biography -
Juvenile literature 3. Engineering - Great Britain -
History - 19th century - Juvenile literature
    I. Title
    624'.092
ISBN 978 0 7502 5195 2

Printed in China
Wayland is a division of Hachette Children's Books, an Hachette Livre UK Company.

For permission to reproduce the following pictures, the author and publisher would like to
thank: Bristol City Museum & Art Gallery, UK/Bridgeman Art Library, London: 4,
Cover; Bristol University, Avon, UK/Bridgeman Art Library, London: 16; City of
London/HIP/TopFoto: 7; Robert Estall/Alamy Images: 20; Getty Images (Hulton
Archive): 14; Martyn Goddard/Corbis: 19, 21; Jason Hawkes/Corbis: 10; Institution of Civil
Engineers, London/Bridgeman Art Library, London: 17; Ironbridge Gorge Museum,
Telford, Shropshire, UK/Bridgeman Art Library, London: 8; Jarrold Publishing/The Art
Archive: 15; Stan Kujawa/Alamy Images: 11; Manor Photography/Alamy Images: 13
National Portrait Gallery, London: 6; Parker Gallery, London/Eileen Tweedy/The Art
Archive: 5; Private Collection/Bridgeman Art Library, London: 12; Private Collection/The
Stapleton Collection/Bridgeman Art Library, London: 18; Ann Ronan Picture
Library/HIP/TopFoto: 9

Contents

Words in **bold** can be found in the glossary.

Who was Brunel?

Isambard Kingdom Brunel was one of Britain's greatest **engineers**. He lived from 1806 to 1859. During his short life, he built many tunnels, bridges, railway lines and stations.

This picture of Isambard Kingdom Brunel was painted in 1843.

Brunel was famous for his iron steamships as well as his **structures**.

Brunel was clever, hard-working and full of brilliant ideas. If something could not be done, he would invent a brand new way of doing it. Often, he worked on structures that others said were impossible to build.

Places to Visit

Brunel **designed** Paddington Station in London and Bristol Temple Meads Station.

Young Brunel

Brunel was born in Portsmouth in 1806. His father was a famous French **engineer** called Marc Isambard Brunel. Before she married his mother's maiden name was Kingdom.

Sir Marc Isambard Brunel, Brunel's father and another great engineer.

At the age of 14, Brunel was sent to school in France. There, he studied maths and science. He returned to England two years later and started work with his father on the Thames Tunnel.

Places to Visit

The Brunel Engine House is a museum that includes the Thames Tunnel. Isambard and his father both worked here.

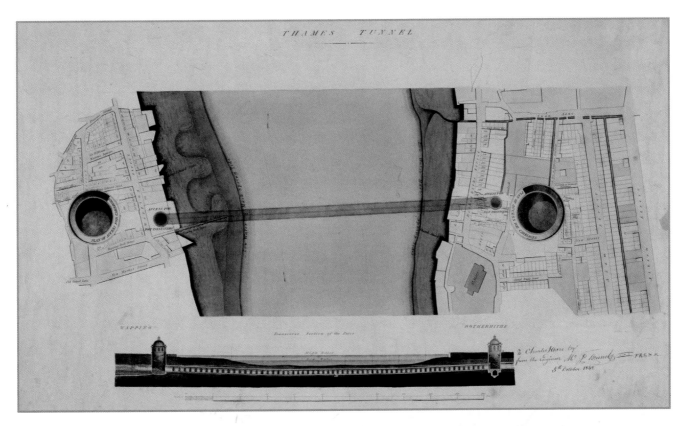

The plan of the Thames Tunnel which was **designed** by Sir Marc Brunel.

The Thames Tunnel

Brunel's first job was building the Thames Tunnel. It was his father's project, but Isambard was in charge of the workers. The Thames Tunnel was the first tunnel in the world to run under a river.

A banquet was held in the Thames Tunnel while it was being built.

In 1828, there was a terrible accident.
Water suddenly burst into the tunnel.
A huge wave washed Brunel from a
platform and hurled him into the water.
He was rescued but was badly injured.

Two people died when
the Thames Tunnel flooded
while it was being built.

Brunel's bridges

In 1830, Brunel won a competition to **design** a bridge. It would be over 200 metres long. It would hang high above the River Avon in Clifton, Bristol. Sadly, Brunel did not live to see his bridge built.

The Clifton Suspension Bridge in Bristol.

Brunel designed and built the Maidenhead Railway Bridge. It has two of the widest, flattest, brick **arches** ever. People were worried that it would fall down, but it did not.

No one believed that the Maidenhead Railway Bridge would be strong enough to carry the weight of a train.

The Great Western Railway

Brunel was the chief **engineer** on the railway between London and Bristol. He decided to follow the flattest route possible. The Great Western Railway was nicknamed 'Brunel's **Billiard Table**' because it was so flat.

When it was built, the Box Tunnel between Bath and Swindon was the longest railway tunnel in the world.

Wide tracks were laid to carry the trains. Brunel believed that these were better and safer than narrow tracks. He thought the journey was smoother, too.

Places to Visit

The Swindon Steam Railway Museum tells the story of the Great Western Railway.

Swindon was a very important stop on the Great Western Railway. This is where they made the trains.

Across the Atlantic

Once he had built a railway from London to Bristol, Brunel was keen to do more. He wanted to transport passengers to the USA, too. So he **designed** and built new ships to carry them across the Atlantic.

Brunel, standing before the huge chains used to slow down the *Great Eastern* ship during its launch.

The *Great Western* was powered by sails and steam. It travelled twice as fast as a sailing boat. Next, Brunel built the first iron steamship. It was called the *SS Great Britain*.

You can visit the *SS Great Britain* in Bristol at Great Western Dock.

A hard worker

Brunel loved his job. He worked long hours and rarely went on holiday. When he married, the family lived in the rooms above his offices in London.

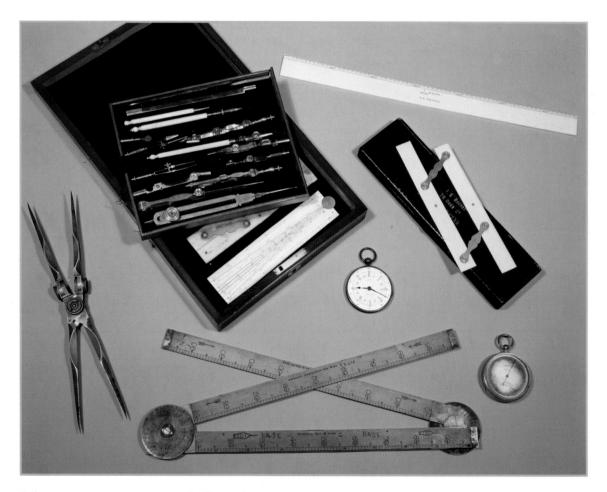

Here are some of the drawing instruments Brunel used to **design** his **structures**.

As well as doing his job, Brunel was also the vice-president of the Institution of Civil Engineers. Sadly, he died before he could become president.

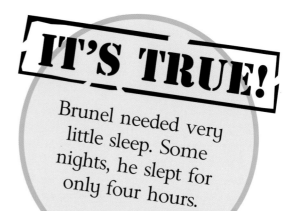

Brunel meeting with Robert Stephenson and other **engineers** to discuss the Britannia Bridge over the Menai Strait in Wales.

Brunel's death

Isambard Kingdom Brunel died in 1859. He was just 53 years old. A few days later, the *Great Eastern* made her maiden voyage to New York City.

The *Great Eastern* was later used to lay a **telegraph cable** across the seabed of the Atlantic Ocean.

After Brunel's death, his fellow **engineers** decided to **honour** him. They started work again on the bridge he **designed**. Brunel's Clifton Suspension Bridge was completed five years later.

The Clifton Suspension Bridge carries traffic 76 metres above the River Avon in Bristol.

After Brunel

Many of the **structures** Brunel built are still used today. His bridges, tunnels, viaducts, railways and docks are there for all to see. They prove how brilliant an **engineer** he was.

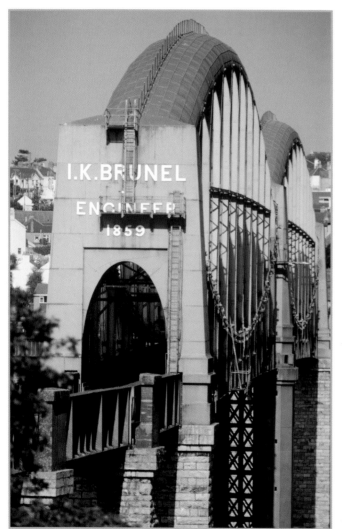

The Royal Albert Bridge at Saltash is one of Brunel's famous bridges.

The firework display over the Clifton Suspension Bridge was magnificent.

In 2006, there were special events and concerts in Bristol to **celebrate** the 200th anniversary of Brunel's birth.

Timeline

1806	Isambard Kingdom Brunel is born on 9 April
1825	Work begins on the Thames Tunnel
1828	Injured in an accident in the Thames Tunnel
1830	Wins the competition to build the Clifton Suspension Bridge
1836	Marries Mary Horsley
1837	The Great Western steamship is launched
1838	The Maidenhead Railway Bridge is completed
1841	The Great Western Railway is opened from London to Bristol
1843	The Thames Tunnel is opened The SS Great Britain is launched
1858	The Great Eastern is launched
1859	The Royal Albert Bridge is opened Brunel dies on 15 September
1864	The Clifton Suspension Bridge is opened
1970	The SS Great Britain is returned to Bristol
2006	Many people celebrate the 200th anniversary of Brunel's birth

Glossary

arch a curved part of a bridge, building or wall

billiard table a flat cloth-covered table on which people play a game with three balls.

celebrate to do something special on an important day

design to draw a plan for something

dock a place where ships and boats are loaded, unloaded or mended

engineer someone who makes machines, or plans the building of roads and bridges

honour to show someone great respect

maiden name a woman's surname before she is married

maiden voyage the very first trip that a ship makes

structure anything that has been built

telegraph cable wires used for sending messages

Further information

Books

The Life of Isambard Kingdom Brunel by Emma Lynch (Heinemann Library, 2006)

Tell me about Isambard Kingdom Brunel by John Malam (Evans Brothers, 1996)

Websites

http://www.bbc.co.uk/schools/famouspeople/standard/brunel/index.shtml

The BBC schools interactive learning website packed with information and quizzes about Brunel.

http://www.brunelenginehouse.org.uk

The Brunel Museum website has lots of photographs of the structures that Brunel planned and built.

Index